Gemini AI: The Power Behind the Next Wave of Tech Disruption

Why This Groundbreaking AI Is a Must-Know for Every Tech Enthusiast

TABLE OF CONTENTS

- **Chapter 4: Innovators' Guide to Integrating Gemini AI**

- Practical Applications and Use Cases for Innovators

- Setting Up Gemini AI for Your Tech Project

- Overcoming Common Integration Challenges

- **Chapter 5: Enhancing Creativity and Innovation with Gemini AI**

- Empowering Developers and Creators

- Using Gemini AI to Fuel New Ideas and Solutions

- Case Studies of Successful Innovators Leveraging Gemini AI

- **Chapter 6: Ethical Considerations and the Future of AI Innovation**

- Navigating the Ethical Challenges of Advanced AI

- The Role of AI Regulation in Shaping the Future

- How Innovators Can Lead with Responsibility

INTRODUCTION

The world of technology is ever-changing, with each advancement pushing us toward an increasingly automated and interconnected future. Among the most significant innovations of recent times is Gemini AI, a system that promises to revolutionize the way we interact with machines and how technology influences our daily lives. Developed by some of the brightest minds in artificial intelligence, Gemini AI stands at the frontier of a new technological era. Its creators, inspired by the idea that machines should not only understand the world but also work in harmony with human thought, set out to create something that is both intuitive and transformative. But what exactly is Gemini AI, and why should it matter to those who are keen on the next great leap in technology?

To understand Gemini AI, it's essential to first take a look at what it is designed to do. At its core, Gemini AI is an advanced form of artificial intelligence capable of performing complex tasks across a variety of fields, from data analysis and natural language processing to more creative and abstract thinking. Unlike earlier forms of AI, which were limited to predefined commands or tasks, Gemini AI operates with a higher level of autonomy and intelligence, allowing it to learn from its environment and adapt to new situations with minimal human intervention.

The creation of Gemini AI was no small feat. It draws upon decades of work in machine learning, neural networks, and deep learning. These areas of study have made it possible to design systems that go beyond simply executing instructions. Instead, they analyze patterns, make predictions, and even generate solutions to problems that might not have clear answers. This makes Gemini AI a particularly powerful tool for industries that rely on the interpretation of large amounts of data, such as healthcare, finance, and technology development.

One of the defining features of Gemini AI is its ability to process information at an unparalleled speed. This, combined with its ability to learn continuously, allows it to outpace traditional forms of automation. Where older systems would require manual adjustments or reprogramming when facing unfamiliar situations, Gemini AI can process new data and adapt without external help, making it a valuable asset for businesses and individuals alike. The potential applications of such a system are nearly limitless, with potential uses in everything from self-driving cars to predictive healthcare. Despite its power, Gemini AI is not merely a tool for large corporations or tech giants. Its accessibility makes it a valuable asset for smaller enterprises and even individuals interested in harnessing the potential of AI. For businesses, the system can provide actionable insights, automate routine tasks, and streamline decision-making processes. For innovators, it opens up a world of possibilities, allowing them to explore new ideas, create novel solutions, and break free from the constraints of traditional software development.

What sets Gemini AI apart from other AI systems is its ability to function in a variety of contexts and industries. It doesn't just excel in one area; its flexibility allows it to be deployed in numerous applications, making it a truly universal tool for innovators. Whether it's helping a startup create a new app or assisting a researcher in analyzing complex data sets, Gemini AI adapts to the needs of its users. This wide-ranging functionality is what makes it such a powerful force in the world of technology.

The convergence of speed, adaptability, and intelligence is something that has been years in the making, and its implications are only beginning to be fully understood. One example of Gemini AI's versatility can be seen in its use in healthcare. With its ability to analyze vast amounts of medical data, Gemini AI is helping doctors make more informed decisions, identify patterns that might have gone unnoticed by human eyes, and even suggest treatment options that would otherwise be overlooked. Imagine a doctor being able to quickly analyze thousands of medical records, imaging scans, and genetic data points to arrive at a diagnosis. This is the promise of Gemini AI— bringing advanced analytics and decision-making capabilities to fields that directly impact people's lives. But as with any powerful technology, there are concerns. The rise of AI has raised questions about data privacy, security, and the future of human labor. Some fear that as machines become more capable, jobs that were once performed by humans will be replaced by automation. Others worry that the vast amounts of data required to train such systems could be misused or lead to privacy violations. These concerns are not without merit, and addressing them will require careful planning and regulation. However, Gemini AI's creators are aware of these issues and have worked to build a system that emphasizes transparency, fairness, and ethical use. Ensuring that the technology serves the greater good while minimizing potential harm will be one of the defining challenges in the years to come.

Moreover, the potential of Gemini AI extends beyond practical applications in fields like healthcare or business. It represents a shift in how we interact with technology as a whole. In many ways, we are moving from a world where machines follow our instructions to one where machines can work alongside us, providing insights, suggestions, and even creating new solutions. This collaborative relationship between humans and machines has the potential to transform industries, enhance productivity, and drive creativity to new heights. As we continue to witness the rise of AI, it is crucial to consider not just the technical capabilities of systems like Gemini AI, but also the societal implications. How will AI affect the job market? What does it mean for the future of human creativity and problem-solving? How do we ensure that AI benefits all of society, rather than a select few? These are questions that will shape the direction of technology in the years ahead, and as Gemini AI continues to evolve, they will remain at the forefront of the conversation.

For tech enthusiasts and innovators, Gemini AI presents an exciting frontier. It offers new opportunities to push the boundaries of what is possible and to explore uncharted territory in the realms of automation, artificial intelligence, and machine learning. Whether you are a seasoned developer, a forward-thinking business leader, or someone simply interested in the next wave of technological innovation, Gemini AI represents the cutting edge. Its impact on the world of technology will only grow as its capabilities are expanded, and its influence will continue to reverberate across industries for years to come.

In the end, Gemini AI is not just a tool—it is a vision of the future. A future where machines do not simply follow orders, but instead collaborate with humans to solve problems, create new ideas, and make the world a better place. The next wave of tech disruption is here, and Gemini AI is leading the charge.

Chapter 1

Understanding Gemini AI

At the heart of modern technological advancement lies the convergence of two forces: artificial intelligence and the sheer scope of human ingenuity. One of the most remarkable achievements in this domain is the creation of Gemini AI, a system that represents a leap forward in both the theoretical and practical applications of AI. But what exactly is Gemini AI? What makes it different from the countless other systems that have come before it? To answer these questions, we must first trace the evolution of artificial intelligence itself and understand the unique features that set Gemini AI apart from its predecessors.

What is Gemini AI?

Gemini AI is a powerful, highly adaptable artificial intelligence system that is designed to function seamlessly across a variety of industries and applications. It is the result of years of research, development, and refinement by some of the brightest minds in technology. At its core, Gemini AI is built to solve complex problems and assist in tasks that typically require human intelligence— whether it's processing data, making decisions, or interacting with users. What sets Gemini AI apart from older models is its ability to not only follow predefined commands but to learn, adapt, and even generate solutions to problems it has never encountered before. Unlike traditional AI systems that rely on rigid programming or narrowly defined tasks, Gemini AI is capable of understanding context, processing vast amounts of information, and making predictions with a high degree of accuracy. It can perform tasks that range from complex data analysis to creative problem solving, making it an incredibly versatile tool. Whether it's used in healthcare to analyze patient data or in business to predict market trends, Gemini AI can bring insights that were previously unimaginable.

At the same time, Gemini AI is designed to work in collaboration with humans, enhancing human decision-making rather than replacing it. It allows professionals to tap into its vast computational power, giving them the ability to address challenges with far greater speed and precision than ever before. Gemini AI is not just a tool—it is a partner in the process of solving some of the most pressing problems in today's world.

The Evolution of AI and Its Impact on Technology

To fully understand Gemini AI, we must take a step back and look at the broader trajectory of artificial intelligence. The field of AI has its roots in the mid-20th century when pioneers like Alan Turing and John McCarthy began exploring the potential for machines to perform tasks traditionally reserved for humans. These early ideas laid the groundwork for what would eventually become a sprawling industry, one that would see waves of optimism followed by periods of disappointment, but ultimately lead to the AI-driven breakthroughs we see today.

In its early stages, AI was primarily based on rule-based systems and symbolic reasoning. These machines could perform specific tasks—like playing chess or solving mathematical problems—by following a set of pre-programmed instructions. However, they were limited in scope and unable to adapt to new situations. The breakthrough came with the development of machine learning, a technique that enabled machines to learn from data rather than simply following a set of predefined rules. By feeding large amounts of data into a system, machines could recognize patterns, make predictions, and improve their performance over time. This marked a significant shift, turning AI into a far more powerful tool for problem-solving.

Over time, machine learning evolved into deep learning, a subset of AI that uses neural networks to mimic the way the human brain processes information. Deep learning systems could analyze even larger and more complex datasets, enabling them to perform tasks like image recognition, speech processing, and language translation with remarkable accuracy. The advent of deep learning opened up new possibilities, allowing AI to be applied to a broader range of fields, from autonomous vehicles to medical diagnostics.

Gemini AI represents the latest evolution in this long-running journey. It combines the best of machine learning and deep learning with an emphasis on adaptability and real-time learning. Where previous AI systems were limited by their training data, Gemini AI can process data in real time, constantly updating its knowledge base to reflect new insights. This ability to learn continuously and adapt quickly to new challenges sets Gemini AI apart as a tool that is not only reactive but also proactive—constantly seeking out new opportunities to improve and optimize.

The impact of AI on technology has been profound. From transforming industries like healthcare, finance, and manufacturing, to reshaping everyday experiences through smart devices and virtual assistants, AI has revolutionized the way we live and work. Its ability to process vast amounts of information quickly has made it indispensable for data-driven decision-making, while its growing presence in automation is transforming the global workforce. As AI continues to evolve, its influence will only deepen, with systems like Gemini AI leading the charge.

Key Features that Make Gemini AI Stand Out

While there are many AI systems on the market today, few can match the capabilities of Gemini AI. Several key features set it apart from its predecessors and place it at the forefront of the next wave of technological innovation.

1. Adaptability

One of the most important characteristics of Gemini AI is its adaptability. Unlike earlier systems that required extensive retraining or manual intervention when faced with new data, Gemini AI is built to learn and adjust in real time. This means that it can process new information as it arrives, making it far more efficient and responsive. Whether it's analyzing a new dataset or adapting to shifting market conditions, Gemini AI can adjust its approach on the fly, making it a far more dynamic tool for innovation.

2. Advanced Natural Language Processing (NLP)

Gemini AI excels in its ability to understand and process natural language, a critical component for systems designed to interact with humans. While earlier AI models could process text data, Gemini AI's natural language processing capabilities are far more advanced. It can understand context, nuance, and even subtle cues in language, allowing for more meaningful and accurate interactions with users. This makes it a powerful tool for applications ranging from customer service to content creation, as it can seamlessly interact with humans in a way that feels natural and intuitive.

3. High-Speed Data Processing

Another feature that sets Gemini AI apart is its incredible processing speed. It is capable of analyzing and processing vast amounts of data in seconds, making it a powerful tool for industries that rely on fast decision-making. In fields like finance, where real-time data is essential, Gemini AI can sift through mountains of information and deliver insights that would otherwise take hours or even days to uncover. This speed allows businesses and individuals to act quickly, gaining a competitive edge in an increasingly fast-paced world.

4. Creativity and Innovation

While many AI systems excel in automation and data analysis, Gemini AI goes a step further by fostering creativity and innovation. It has been designed to generate new ideas, offering suggestions and solutions to problems that might not be immediately apparent. Whether it's creating a new marketing strategy or designing a groundbreaking piece of technology, Gemini AI can help users think outside the box and push the boundaries of what's possible.

5. Ethical Considerations and Transparency

As AI becomes more integrated into society, questions about ethics and transparency become increasingly important. The developers behind Gemini AI have placed a strong emphasis on creating a system that operates with integrity and fairness. From ensuring that data is handled securely to implementing safeguards against bias, Gemini AI is built to operate responsibly in the real world. It is not simply a tool for profit but a system designed to benefit society as a whole.

In conclusion, Gemini AI represents the cutting edge of artificial intelligence, combining speed, adaptability, and creativity in a way that previous systems could only dream of. As we continue to explore the capabilities of this powerful tool, its potential to reshape industries and improve lives is only just beginning to unfold.

Chapter 2

How Gemini AI Works: The Science Behind the System

At its core, artificial intelligence is built upon the intricate interplay of algorithms, data, and computation. Each advancement in AI, each breakthrough that pushes the boundaries of what machines can accomplish, is a product of decades of research and refinement. The true marvel of Gemini AI lies in its ability to synthesize multiple technologies and approaches—combining them into a unified system that can not only process data but understand it, adapt to it, and generate meaningful results. To truly appreciate how Gemini AI works, we need to explore the core technologies that make it tick, from the foundational algorithms to the deep learning systems that power its intelligence.

Core Technologies and Algorithms

At the heart of any AI system are the algorithms that enable it to make decisions, recognize patterns, and optimize its performance. These algorithms are not simply a set of instructions; they are the underlying logic that governs how a machine processes data and learns from its environment.

Gemini AI is built on a set of advanced algorithms that allow it to handle a wide variety of tasks, from simple decision-making processes to more complex problem-solving scenarios. These algorithms are the framework through which Gemini AI learns to interpret data, adapt to new situations, and perform tasks with increasing accuracy over time. A key feature of Gemini AI's algorithmic approach is its ability to continuously update itself. In traditional systems, algorithms are static—once they are programmed, they function in the same way regardless of new data or changing conditions. Gemini AI, however, operates through dynamic algorithms that evolve in response to new information. As the system processes more data, its algorithms adjust to account for new patterns, insights, or errors. This constant evolution allows Gemini AI to function in a variety of environments, from real-time decision-making in fast-paced industries to more nuanced applications in healthcare or research.

One of the most important sets of algorithms in Gemini AI is its optimization algorithms. These algorithms are designed to improve the system's performance over time. Whether Gemini AI is optimizing an existing process, predicting future trends, or enhancing a solution based on user feedback, the optimization algorithms guide the system toward more effective outcomes. This process of continuous optimization is what gives Gemini AI its edge—constantly refining its models and predictions based on incoming data and shifting requirements.

Machine Learning and Deep Learning in Gemini AI

Machine learning (ML) and deep learning (DL) are at the heart of many modern AI systems, and Gemini AI is no exception. These two subfields of AI focus on how machines can learn from data and improve their performance without being explicitly programmed to do so. However, while they are often used interchangeably, machine learning and deep learning are distinct techniques with different levels of complexity and capability.

> Machine Learning : At its core, machine learning involves training a system to

recognize patterns in data. Instead of relying on hand-coded rules, ML systems learn from historical data to identify patterns, make predictions, and improve over time. Machine learning in Gemini AI is used to analyze vast datasets, extract valuable insights, and enable the system to make informed decisions. It allows the system to adapt as it encounters new data, becoming more accurate with each iteration. For instance, in a predictive model for stock market trends, Gemini AI could use historical data to predict future movements, continuously improving its accuracy as new data is incorporated into the system. One of the most important types of machine learning used in Gemini AI is supervised learning , where the system is trained using labeled datasets. These datasets contain both input data (such as a set of images) and output data (the correct label for each image). The machine learns to map inputs to the correct output, and with enough examples, it can generalize this knowledge to new, unseen data. This is essential for tasks like classification or regression, where accurate predictions are critical.

> Deep Learning : Deep learning, a subset of machine learning, takes things a step further by using neural networks with many layers. These multilayered neural networks, often referred to as "deep neural networks," are designed to simulate the way the human brain processes information. Deep learning is particularly well-suited for tasks that involve unstructured data, such as images, audio, or text, where traditional machine learning approaches may fall short.

In Gemini AI, deep learning models are used to extract higher-level features from raw data, enabling the system to understand complex relationships that might be too difficult for conventional algorithms to handle. For example, in image recognition, deep learning allows Gemini AI to identify objects in an image by processing each layer of the neural network—starting from basic edges and shapes and progressing to more complex structures like faces, animals, or vehicles. This hierarchical approach is what gives deep learning its power, and it is why Gemini AI can handle such a wide range of tasks.

One of the breakthroughs in deep learning is the use of convolutional neural networks (CNNs) , which are specifically designed for image processing. CNNs allow Gemini AI to understand visual data at multiple levels of abstraction, making them invaluable in fields like healthcare (for medical imaging), automotive (for autonomous driving), and entertainment (for visual effects and media recognition). The combination of machine learning and deep learning allows Gemini AI to not only recognize patterns but to build complex models that can generalize across a range of tasks. The ability to process both structured and unstructured data with equal proficiency is what makes Gemini AI such a versatile and powerful tool.

Neural Networks and Natural Language Processing

The two key technologies that truly enable Gemini AI to interact with humans in a meaningful way are neural networks and natural language processing (NLP) . Both are essential to the system's ability to interpret and generate human-like communication, whether through text, speech, or other forms of interaction.

> Neural Networks : Neural networks are the backbone of both machine learning and deep

learning systems. Inspired by the way neurons in the human brain communicate with each other, neural networks are made up of layers of interconnected nodes (or "neurons"), each performing simple mathematical functions. These nodes work together to process information and make decisions. The more layers a neural network has, the deeper and more complex the relationships it can learn.

In Gemini AI, neural networks are used to process data, detect patterns, and make decisions. Whether it's recognizing speech, understanding images, or predicting trends, neural networks are the foundation that allows the system to learn from data in a highly efficient and flexible way. This is particularly crucial for tasks that require a high degree of accuracy and nuance, such as medical diagnoses, legal document analysis, or customer service chatbots.

> Natural Language Processing (NLP): Language is one of the most complex forms of human communication, and for AI to truly interact with people, it must be able to understand and generate natural language. Natural language processing, or NLP, is the branch of AI that focuses on how machines can process and understand human language.

Gemini AI's NLP capabilities are state-of-the-art, enabling it to understand context, tone, and meaning in text and speech. From text classification to sentiment analysis, Gemini AI can handle a wide range of NLP tasks. More advanced capabilities, such as machine translation and speech recognition, allow it to operate in real-time, providing dynamic interactions that feel natural to users.

The combination of neural networks and NLP is what allows Gemini AI to engage in meaningful conversations, understand questions, and generate accurate responses. Whether it's answering queries, summarizing information, or holding intelligent discussions, Gemini AI can process language in ways that are indistinguishable from human interaction.

The inner workings of Gemini AI are rooted in the complex science of algorithms, machine learning, deep learning, neural networks, and natural language processing. Together, these technologies form the foundation of a system capable of learning, adapting, and improving in ways that were once reserved for human intelligence. Gemini AI is not simply a tool for automation; it is a partner in the process of understanding, problem-solving, and innovation. As the system continues to evolve, its potential will expand, opening new frontiers in technology and human-machine collaboration.

Chapter 3

The Role of Gemini AI in Tech Disruption

In the vast landscape of technology, few advancements have had the potential to disrupt industries as profoundly as artificial intelligence. Among the leaders of this revolution is Gemini AI, a system that has shown itself capable of transforming entire sectors. From healthcare to finance, its impact is already being felt, and the trajectory suggests that its influence will only grow. But the reach of Gemini AI extends beyond just these fields. Its ability to integrate into automation processes and its implications for data security and privacy also mark it as a disruptive force that is reshaping the modern technological world. Understanding how Gemini AI fits into the broader tech disruption narrative requires a look at its influence across multiple industries and its broader societal implications.

Transforming Industries: From Healthcare to Finance

One of the most striking features of Gemini AI is its adaptability. While many technologies are specialized, excelling in one area but struggling to extend beyond that, Gemini AI's versatility allows it to be applied across a wide range of industries. Nowhere is this more apparent than in its transformative effect on sectors such as healthcare and finance—two industries that directly impact human lives and economic stability.

> Healthcare: The healthcare sector has long been burdened with challenges related to efficiency, accuracy, and the ability to process massive amounts of data. Gemini AI is beginning to address these challenges by

making healthcare more personalized, accessible, and effective. For example, in medical imaging, Gemini AI can assist doctors by analyzing X-rays, CT scans, and MRIs with incredible precision. Rather than simply identifying anomalies, the AI system can learn from vast datasets of medical images to predict potential conditions, flagging concerns that might otherwise be overlooked. In diagnostics, Gemini AI has the ability to analyze patient data—ranging from medical history to genetic information—and identify patterns that suggest the likelihood of certain diseases. This ability to process both structured and unstructured data, while continually learning and adapting, enables doctors to make more informed decisions faster. In the realm of drug discovery, the AI system can assist researchers by sifting through vast chemical databases to identify promising compounds, significantly speeding up the discovery of new treatments and therapies.

Moreover, the integration of Gemini AI into the healthcare system can enhance patient outcomes. Real-time data analysis allows for quicker reactions to critical changes in a patient's condition, improving survival rates and reducing errors. The AI's ability to constantly learn from new cases and medical advancements ensures that it remains on the cutting edge, delivering up-to-date insights to healthcare professionals.

> Finance: The financial industry has always been a hotbed for technological disruption, and AI, particularly systems like Gemini AI, has proven to be a game-changer. With its ability to process vast amounts of data in real time, Gemini AI can analyze market trends, assess risk, and optimize investment strategies with unparalleled efficiency. For example, investment firms are increasingly turning to AI systems to manage portfolios.

By leveraging Gemini AI, these firms can not only automate routine tasks like data collection and transaction execution but also tap into advanced predictive models that analyze everything from historical market movements to geopolitical events. The result is a more responsive, accurate, and dynamic approach to managing investments.

In banking, Gemini AI can be used to detect fraudulent activity by analyzing transaction patterns in real time. By identifying discrepancies and flagging potentially suspicious behavior, the system helps prevent financial crimes before they escalate. Similarly, credit scoring has traditionally been a complex, somewhat opaque process. Gemini AI can offer a more personalized and accurate evaluation by considering a wider range of data sources, making the system more inclusive and efficient.

Gemini AI's potential in the financial sector extends to customer service as well. Financial institutions are employing AI-driven chatbots and virtual assistants powered by Gemini AI to provide customers with personalized advice, handle queries, and guide them through financial decisions. These AI systems are not limited to simple scripted interactions but instead use deep learning to offer nuanced, human-like assistance, further blurring the line between human expertise and machine efficiency.

Gemini AI and Its Influence on Automation

The role of automation in reshaping industries is no longer a prediction—it is a present-day reality. Across the board, businesses are looking for ways to increase efficiency, cut costs, and streamline operations. AI, particularly systems like Gemini AI, is playing a central role in this transformation.

From manufacturing plants to service industries, Gemini AI's integration into automation processes promises significant productivity gains. In manufacturing, AI-driven robots powered by Gemini AI can handle tasks that would otherwise require human labor. Whether it's assembling components, conducting quality control, or monitoring machinery, AI can manage these processes with precision, consistency, and speed, reducing human error and improving overall efficiency. In the realm of logistics, Gemini AI is helping companies optimize their supply chains. It can predict demand for products, track inventory in real time, and automatically adjust orders to ensure timely delivery. By analyzing past trends and current data, the system can anticipate potential disruptions—whether it's a delay in shipping or a supply shortage—and adjust operations to minimize their impact. But the effects of automation aren't limited to industries with physical labor. In sectors like customer service, AI is automating processes that were once considered too complex for machines. Gemini AI can handle everything from processing customer complaints to providing personalized recommendations, allowing companies to provide 24/7 service without the need for a large human workforce. This not only cuts costs but also frees up human employees to focus on more complex, high-value tasks.

Automation driven by Gemini AI isn't just about reducing costs—it's also about creating new opportunities. By automating routine tasks, companies can reallocate resources to innovation and research, exploring new ways to grow and expand their businesses. The AI-driven insights provided by Gemini AI also allow businesses to better understand customer preferences, industry trends, and market dynamics, opening up new avenues for growth.

Impact on Data Security and Privacy

While the benefits of Gemini AI in fields like healthcare, finance, and automation are clear, the technology also brings with it significant challenges, particularly in the areas of data security and privacy. As AI systems increasingly take on roles that require the handling of sensitive information, the question of how to secure that data becomes paramount.

Gemini AI's ability to process vast amounts of data quickly and efficiently makes it a valuable tool for businesses and institutions that rely on data-driven decisions. However, this same capacity also raises concerns about data breaches, unauthorized access, and the misuse of sensitive information. To address these concerns, developers have built Gemini AI with robust security protocols, ensuring that all data handled by the system is encrypted, protected, and subject to strict access controls. But as the system becomes more pervasive, so too does the risk.

One of the key challenges with AI in general is that it often requires access to large datasets to function effectively. This can include everything from personal health records to financial transactions, raising serious concerns about privacy. How much of our personal data should be available to AI systems, and who is responsible for ensuring that this data is not exploited? These questions are central to ongoing debates about AI ethics and regulation.

In the case of Gemini AI, developers are focusing on transparency and accountability. The system is designed with clear data management practices, giving users control over their data and ensuring that it is only used for the purposes it was intended for. Furthermore, continuous audits and updates are implemented to safeguard against vulnerabilities and ensure that the system remains compliant with evolving data protection regulations worldwide.

Gemini AI's role in securing data is not limited to protecting it from external threats. The system can also be used to enhance cybersecurity efforts by detecting anomalous behavior, identifying potential threats, and responding in real time. By continuously learning from new threats, Gemini AI can help organizations stay one step ahead of cybercriminals. Gemini AI is more than just a technological advancement; it is a force that is reshaping industries, automating processes, and raising critical questions about the future of data security and privacy. From healthcare to finance, its impact is already being felt, and as the system continues to evolve, its reach will only grow. As with any transformative technology, the benefits come with challenges, and how society chooses to navigate these challenges will determine the ultimate success of Gemini AI. As the system plays an increasingly prominent role in the future of technology, its potential to disrupt and innovate remains unmatched.

Chapter 4

Innovators' Guide to Integrating Gemini AI

The arrival of Gemini AI signals a new era in technological capabilities, and for innovators, it presents an unprecedented opportunity. The potential of this advanced AI system is vast, offering powerful tools for problem-solving, automation, and data analysis. But as with any revolutionary technology, integrating Gemini AI into a tech project is no simple task. It requires careful planning, an understanding of its practical applications, and strategies to overcome potential hurdles. For those ready to leverage Gemini AI's capabilities, this chapter will explore the steps for successful integration, focusing on real-world applications, the setup process, and how to navigate the challenges that come with using cutting-edge technology.

Practical Applications and Use Cases for Innovators

Before diving into the technical details of integration, it's essential to understand where and how Gemini AI can be applied. Its flexibility is one of its most powerful attributes, allowing it to enhance a wide range of industries and applications. Innovators can harness Gemini AI to transform existing systems, develop new products, or streamline operations in ways that were previously unthinkable. The following use cases highlight the diverse potential Gemini AI offers to innovators.

1. Healthcare

Healthcare is one of the sectors where Gemini AI's impact is already being felt most profoundly. Innovators in the medical field can use Gemini AI to analyze medical data, predict disease outcomes, and assist in diagnostics. By integrating Gemini AI into existing healthcare systems, organizations can improve patient care, streamline administrative tasks, and reduce human error. For instance, Gemini AI can process large sets of medical records to identify early warning signs of conditions such as cancer or heart disease, helping doctors make more accurate diagnoses.

Additionally, the technology can be used for personalized medicine, analyzing patient genetics and lifestyle to recommend specific treatments or interventions. This capability makes Gemini AI an invaluable asset to innovators working in healthcare, whether they are developing new medical devices, software, or improving overall care delivery.

2. Finance

For innovators in the finance industry, Gemini AI offers a wealth of possibilities.

From predictive analytics to fraud detection, AI's ability to process large volumes of financial data in real time allows for more efficient decision-making and risk management. Innovators can integrate Gemini AI into stock trading platforms to predict market trends, helping investors make more informed decisions. Moreover, banks and financial institutions can use Gemini AI to enhance customer service through automated chatbots and virtual assistants, providing personalized advice and support.

The technology's potential also extends to automating complex financial processes, such as loan approval or credit scoring. By integrating Gemini AI into their operations, finance professionals can improve accuracy, reduce processing times, and offer more personalized financial services.

3. Retail and E-commerce

In the retail and e-commerce sectors, Gemini AI can be used to personalize customer experiences, predict trends, and optimize inventory management. For example, AI can analyze consumer behavior to offer targeted recommendations, driving sales and improving customer satisfaction. By integrating Gemini AI into e-commerce platforms, innovators can automate customer service interactions, offering instant support via AI-powered chatbots that can handle inquiries, resolve issues, and recommend products. AI's ability to process large datasets allows retailers to predict demand more accurately, ensuring that products are stocked in the right quantities at the right times. This application can significantly reduce waste and improve profitability.

4. Manufacturing and Supply Chain

In manufacturing, Gemini AI can optimize production lines, monitor quality control, and predict equipment failure before it happens. By integrating the AI system into the manufacturing process, innovators can ensure that operations are as efficient and cost-effective as possible. In supply chain management, AI can help predict disruptions, optimize delivery routes, and manage inventory more effectively. Gemini AI's ability to analyze vast amounts of data in real-time means it can identify inefficiencies and suggest improvements that might otherwise go unnoticed, ensuring that companies remain competitive in an increasingly fast-paced market.

Setting Up Gemini AI for Your Tech Project

Successfully integrating Gemini AI into a tech project requires careful planning and execution. Whether you are a developer, a business leader, or a tech enthusiast, understanding the steps involved in setting up the system is crucial for a smooth and effective implementation.

1. Identify the Problem to Solve

The first step in setting up Gemini AI for your project is to clearly define the problem or challenge you intend to address. Gemini AI is a tool, and like any tool, it is most effective when used for a specific purpose. Are you trying to improve customer service? Optimize your supply chain? Enhance predictive analytics for decision-making? Identifying the core problem will help you focus on the right features of Gemini AI and tailor its capabilities to meet your needs.

2. Data Collection and Preparation

AI systems rely on data to learn and make predictions, and Gemini AI is no different.

For innovators, this means gathering relevant, high-quality data that will allow the system to function effectively. Data preparation is an often overlooked but critical part of the integration process. The data must be cleaned, organized, and formatted in a way that Gemini AI can process efficiently. If you are working in a sector like healthcare or finance, where data privacy and security are paramount, ensuring that the data you use is compliant with regulations such as HIPAA or GDPR is crucial. The more structured and accurate your data, the better Gemini AI will perform, leading to more reliable outcomes.

3. Integrating Gemini AI into Existing Systems

Once you have identified your problem and prepared the data, the next step is integrating Gemini AI into your existing infrastructure. This involves connecting the

AI system to your databases, software, and other systems that will feed it data. Many companies choose to use APIs to facilitate integration, allowing Gemini AI to pull data from different sources and seamlessly communicate with other software tools. Depending on your industry, there may also be specific integration requirements. For example, in healthcare, Gemini AI may need to work with existing electronic health record (EHR) systems, while in retail, it may need to interface with e-commerce platforms or CRM systems. Careful attention must be paid to ensuring that all systems work together smoothly and that the integration does not disrupt existing operations.

4. Training and Testing

Once Gemini AI is integrated, it is time to begin training the system. Training involves feeding the AI model with large datasets so that it can learn to make predictions or decisions based on patterns in the data. This process may take time, depending on the complexity of the task and the size of the data. Testing is equally important. Before rolling out Gemini AI across your entire operation, you should conduct extensive testing to ensure that the system is working as expected. This may involve running simulations, monitoring the AI's performance, and adjusting the system based on feedback.

Overcoming Common Integration Challenges

While integrating Gemini AI into your project can bring immense benefits, it is not without challenges. Being aware of potential obstacles and understanding how to navigate them can help ensure a smooth and successful integration.

1. Data Quality and Availability

One of the most common hurdles in AI integration is data quality. Gemini AI can only be as good as the data it is fed. Poor-quality, incomplete, or biased data can lead to inaccurate predictions and suboptimal results. To overcome this challenge, innovators must ensure they are collecting clean, reliable data and continually monitoring the system for errors or inconsistencies.

2. Resistance to Change

Introducing AI into an organization can be met with resistance, particularly from employees who fear job displacement or are unfamiliar with the technology. To address this, innovators must engage with their teams early in the process, educating them about the benefits of Gemini AI and how it will complement their work rather than replace it. Building a culture of collaboration between humans and machines is essential for successful integration.

3. Scalability

As your business grows, so too will the demands on Gemini AI. Ensuring that the system is scalable and capable of handling increased data loads and complexity is critical. Innovators must plan for future growth and ensure that Gemini AI can adapt to new challenges as they arise.

Integrating Gemini AI into your tech project presents an exciting opportunity to innovate and revolutionize how you approach problem-solving. By understanding its practical applications, setting it up correctly, and addressing the common challenges that come with AI integration, innovators can unlock the full potential of this powerful system. The road to successful integration may be complex, but with the right planning, support, and approach, Gemini AI can help transform industries, drive efficiency, and open the door to new possibilities.

Chapter 5

Enhancing Creativity and Innovation with Gemini AI

Throughout history, great leaps in innovation have been fueled by new tools and technologies. From the printing press to the personal computer, each breakthrough has empowered creators to explore new ideas and reach audiences in ways previously thought impossible. Today, one of the most exciting tools for innovators is Gemini AI, a system that has the potential to transform the creative process and drive the next wave of technological advancements. Whether you're a developer, designer, artist, or entrepreneur, Gemini AI offers a vast array of capabilities that can help unlock new possibilities and bring your ideas to life. This chapter explores how Gemini AI can enhance creativity, foster innovation, and support the next generation of thinkers and creators.

Empowering Developers and Creators

At its heart, Gemini AI is a tool designed to amplify human creativity. For developers, it acts as a partner in the coding process, streamlining complex tasks and offering insights that can enhance their work. Whether you're building a new application, designing a website, or developing software for an entirely new field, Gemini AI can assist in every stage of development.

1. Code Generation and Optimization

One of the primary ways that Gemini AI empowers developers is through its ability to generate code. Traditionally, writing code can be a time-consuming process, with developers having to troubleshoot errors, optimize for performance, and ensure that everything functions as intended. Gemini AI can assist in generating initial code structures based on specific requirements, significantly speeding up the development process. By analyzing vast amounts of code from previous projects, Gemini AI can suggest efficient code snippets, identify potential bugs, and recommend optimizations that might not be immediately obvious.

For instance, when developing an application, a developer can use Gemini AI to automatically generate boilerplate code or even write functions based on natural language instructions. This allows developers to focus more on high-level problem-solving and design while leaving routine coding tasks to the AI system. Additionally, as the system continuously learns from previous code, it becomes increasingly adept at offering contextually relevant suggestions, further enhancing productivity.

2. Enhancing Collaboration

In team-based environments, collaboration is key. Gemini AI enables seamless collaboration between developers and other stakeholders, such as designers, product managers, and marketers. The AI's ability to process and synthesize information makes it an invaluable tool for teams working on complex projects. Developers can use Gemini AI to quickly understand design specifications or user requirements and ensure that the code they write aligns with the broader vision of the product.

For creators in the design space, Gemini AI can assist in generating design prototypes, suggesting layouts, and offering feedback based on user experience principles. By integrating the AI into the creative workflow, designers can iterate faster and focus on pushing boundaries rather than getting bogged down by repetitive tasks.

Using Gemini AI to Fuel New Ideas and Solutions

While Gemini AI is undoubtedly a powerful tool for speeding up workflows and improving efficiency, its true potential lies in its ability to fuel creativity and innovation. AI systems like Gemini have the capacity to not only generate content and ideas but also to act as a creative partner, helping human creators unlock new solutions that may not have been previously considered.

1. Idea Generation

At its core, innovation is about thinking outside the box and approaching problems from a new perspective. One of the ways that Gemini AI helps spark creativity is by offering novel solutions to complex problems. For instance, innovators in industries like marketing or product design can input a challenge or set of parameters into Gemini AI, and the system will generate a variety of possible solutions. These solutions might range from new marketing campaigns to innovative product features or unique business strategies. For example, a product designer could ask Gemini AI to suggest innovative ways to improve an existing product. The AI might analyze previous iterations of the product, customer reviews, and industry trends, then provide new design ideas or features that could set the product apart from the competition. This approach not only accelerates the ideation phase but also ensures that the ideas are informed by data and real-world insights.

2. Creative Assistance

Gemini AI's role in fueling creativity goes beyond just idea generation. It can also help creators push the boundaries of their fields. In music, for instance, AI-powered tools can assist composers in generating new melodies, harmonies, and arrangements. Writers can use AI to craft compelling storylines, generate dialogue, or overcome writer's block. Visual artists can turn to AI to explore new art styles, generate concepts, or manipulate images in ways that would take hours or even days for a human artist to complete manually. Gemini AI's ability to analyze existing works, identify trends, and learn from a vast array of sources means it can offer suggestions that might otherwise be overlooked. In film, it can help screenwriters craft engaging narratives by analyzing character arcs, plot structure, and pacing. In architecture, AI can suggest new building designs or efficient layouts based on a client's preferences, available materials, and environmental considerations. Whether you are working on a new novel, painting, app design, or even a business model, Gemini AI offers the potential to spark innovation and break through creative barriers.

3. Solving Complex Problems

Creativity is not just about creating new things—it's also about solving problems. Gemini AI's capacity for complex data analysis makes it an invaluable tool for innovators working on challenging problems. Whether in the sciences, engineering, or social entrepreneurship, Gemini AI can analyze vast amounts of data, identify patterns, and suggest solutions to problems that might take human researchers months or years to discover. For example, in the field of climate science, Gemini AI can assist in developing models to predict the effects of climate change and suggest mitigation strategies. In social entrepreneurship, innovators can use Gemini AI to assess the effectiveness of potential solutions to issues like poverty, inequality, or access to education, drawing on data from around the world to inform their decisions.

Case Studies of Successful Innovators Leveraging Gemini AI

While the potential for Gemini AI to drive innovation is clear, its real-world applications have already begun to make waves across various industries. Let's take a look at some case studies of innovators who have successfully harnessed the power of Gemini AI to enhance creativity, improve efficiency, and develop new solutions.

1. Innovating in Healthcare: Personalized Treatment Plans

In the healthcare industry, an innovative team of doctors and data scientists turned to Gemini AI to create personalized treatment plans for cancer patients. By analyzing vast amounts of patient data, including medical records, genetic information, and treatment history, the AI system was able to suggest treatment regimens tailored to each individual's needs. The system also flagged potential drug interactions and side effects, helping doctors make more informed decisions.

This approach not only improved patient outcomes but also sped up the decision-making process, allowing healthcare professionals to provide more targeted care in less time. The team's success was largely attributed to Gemini AI's ability to synthesize complex data and present it in a way that was easily actionable for medical professionals.

2. Redefining Marketing Campaigns: Predictive Analytics for Consumer Behavior

A leading e-commerce company used Gemini AI to transform their marketing strategies. By analyzing vast amounts of consumer data, including browsing history, purchase behavior, and demographic information, Gemini AI helped the company predict which products would be popular at different times of the year. The system also suggested personalized marketing campaigns, improving customer engagement and driving sales.

This shift toward data-driven marketing not only increased the company's profitability but also enhanced customer satisfaction by offering more relevant and timely products. Gemini AI's ability to predict trends and generate insights was instrumental in reshaping the company's approach to marketing and customer engagement.

3. Revolutionizing Product Design: Automating the Creative Process

An innovative startup in the consumer electronics space integrated Gemini AI into its product design process to develop a new type of wearable device. The AI system analyzed consumer preferences, existing market trends, and material properties, then generated design concepts based on this data. The result was a product that combined functionality, style, and user demand in ways that set it apart from the competition.

Gemini AI's role in automating aspects of the design process allowed the team to move from concept to prototype faster than ever before, giving the startup a competitive edge in the fast-moving tech market. The success of the product demonstrated the power of Gemini AI to assist in creative endeavors, turning raw ideas into tangible, market-ready products. Gemini AI represents a leap forward in the world of creativity and innovation. By empowering developers, creators, and entrepreneurs with powerful tools to streamline workflows, generate new ideas, and solve complex problems, Gemini AI is poised to transform industries across the globe. As demonstrated in case studies and real-world applications, the system has already proven its ability to drive creative breakthroughs and deliver tangible results. For those ready to harness its power, Gemini AI offers a world of possibilities—one that can reshape the way we think, create, and innovate.

Chapter 6

Ethical Considerations and the Future of AI Innovation

Artificial intelligence holds the promise of profound societal change, but with that potential comes a deep responsibility. The development of advanced AI systems such as Gemini AI presents unique ethical challenges that cannot be ignored. As AI continues to evolve and play an increasingly central role in our lives, innovators, regulators, and society at large must confront questions surrounding its impact. How do we ensure AI systems are developed responsibly? What safeguards should be in place to protect human rights, privacy, and fairness? This chapter explores these ethical challenges, the evolving role of regulation, and how innovators can take the lead in shaping a future where AI benefits all.

Navigating the Ethical Challenges of Advanced AI

As AI systems like Gemini AI become more capable, they begin to raise a host of ethical questions, especially around issues of fairness, transparency, and accountability. One of the most pressing concerns is how AI systems make decisions. Unlike traditional algorithms, which are generally rule-based and predictable, advanced AI systems like Gemini AI learn from vast amounts of data, often making decisions that even their creators may not fully understand. This can create challenges in ensuring that these systems are fair, unbiased, and aligned with human values.

1. Bias and Fairness

Bias in AI systems is one of the most discussed ethical issues. Machine learning algorithms, including those used by Gemini

AI, are trained on large datasets, and if these datasets contain biases—whether based on race, gender, socioeconomic status, or other factors—the AI system can inadvertently perpetuate and even amplify those biases. For instance, if an AI system trained on historical hiring data learns that certain groups have been underrepresented in a specific profession, it might continue to favor applicants from those groups who historically filled the role, overlooking qualified candidates from other groups.

Addressing this issue requires a concerted effort from developers to ensure that the data used to train AI systems is representative, diverse, and free of harmful biases. It also requires transparency in the development process, with regular audits and assessments to ensure the AI behaves in ways that align with ethical standards. Innovators must build systems that are not only effective but also equitable, ensuring that the technology serves all segments of society fairly.

2. Privacy and Surveillance

Another significant ethical concern with AI is the issue of privacy. As AI systems are used to analyze vast amounts of personal data— from medical records to browsing habits— there is an inherent risk that this data could be misused or accessed without consent. In the wrong hands, AI could become a tool for mass surveillance, threatening individual freedoms and rights to privacy. Gemini AI, for instance, can process enormous amounts of data to derive insights or make predictions. While this is a powerful capability, it also raises questions about how personal information is collected, stored, and used. Innovators must prioritize data security and user consent, ensuring that individuals have control over their information and that their privacy is protected.

AI developers should implement measures such as anonymization, data encryption, and strict data access protocols to mitigate privacy risks. Additionally, as AI systems become more pervasive, society must have open discussions about the balance between the benefits of AI and the need for privacy protections.

3. Autonomy and Human Control

As AI becomes more autonomous, there is a growing concern over human oversight. In certain applications, such as autonomous vehicles or healthcare diagnostics, the stakes are high—decisions made by AI systems could directly impact human lives. Innovators must ensure that AI remains a tool to assist human decision-making, not replace it entirely. While AI systems can process and analyze data more efficiently than humans, they lack the ability to understand context or the nuances of human experience.

The ethical challenge here is finding the right balance. AI should augment human decision-making, not supplant it. Ensuring that humans remain in control, particularly in critical areas such as healthcare or justice, is vital to maintaining ethical standards. Innovators must embed oversight mechanisms into AI systems to ensure that humans can intervene when necessary.

The Role of AI Regulation in Shaping the Future

As AI technologies continue to advance, governments and regulatory bodies are increasingly called upon to define the legal and ethical frameworks within which AI operates. The challenge of regulating AI is complicated by its rapid development and the diverse ways in which it is used. While regulation is necessary to ensure the ethical deployment of AI, it also needs to be flexible enough to allow innovation to flourish.

1. The Need for Global Standards

AI is a global technology, and its impact is felt across borders. As such, there is a growing need for international standards to guide the development and deployment of AI systems. Without these standards, there is a risk that different countries may develop conflicting regulations, creating barriers to collaboration and innovation. Additionally, inconsistent regulations could lead to a "race to the bottom," where companies cut corners on ethical considerations to comply with less stringent laws.

Creating global standards for AI is no easy task, given the diverse cultures, legal systems, and ethical norms across the world. However, international cooperation on AI regulation is critical. Efforts to create global standards, such as the AI guidelines set forth by the European Union, represent a step in the right direction. These guidelines emphasize transparency, accountability, and fairness in AI development and aim to ensure that AI is used in ways that benefit society as a whole.

2. Regulation vs. Innovation

One of the key challenges in AI regulation is striking a balance between protecting society and fostering innovation. Overly stringent regulations could stifle creativity, making it difficult for developers to experiment with new ideas or push the boundaries of what AI can achieve. Conversely, a lack of regulation could lead to unethical applications of AI, such as in autonomous weapons or mass surveillance systems. Regulation should not be seen as a hindrance to innovation, but rather as a framework to ensure that innovation occurs in a responsible, ethical manner. Regulators and innovators must work together to create policies that protect consumers, preserve privacy, and promote fairness while still encouraging technological progress. This balance will be crucial in shaping the future of AI.

3. Transparency and Accountability in AI

One of the key areas for regulation is ensuring that AI systems are transparent and accountable. As AI becomes more autonomous, it becomes increasingly difficult for users to understand how decisions are made. This lack of transparency can undermine trust in AI systems, particularly in areas like criminal justice, hiring, and lending. Regulatory bodies must ensure that AI developers are transparent about how their systems work, including the data they use and the algorithms that power them. Additionally, there must be mechanisms in place to hold AI developers accountable for the decisions made by their systems. If an AI system causes harm or acts in an unethical manner, there should be clear pathways for redress.

How Innovators Can Lead with Responsibility

While regulation will play a significant role in shaping the future of AI, the responsibility for ethical AI development ultimately rests with the innovators themselves. Developers, designers, and entrepreneurs who work with AI have a unique opportunity to lead by example and create technologies that prioritize fairness, transparency, and accountability.

1. Designing with Ethics in Mind

Ethical considerations should be integrated into the design process from the very beginning. Innovators should consider the potential societal impacts of their technologies and design them to minimize harm. This includes ensuring that AI systems are inclusive, that they do not reinforce existing biases, and that they respect privacy and autonomy. Incorporating ethical principles into the design process requires collaboration between AI developers, ethicists, social scientists, and other stakeholders. These diverse perspectives will ensure that AI systems are not only technically sound but also socially responsible.

2. Creating Inclusive AI Systems

As AI systems become more integral to our daily lives, it is essential that they serve the needs of diverse populations. Innovators must work to ensure that AI systems are accessible and fair to all people, regardless of their race, gender, or socioeconomic status.

This includes designing systems that are sensitive to cultural differences and that can be used by individuals from all backgrounds.

3. Encouraging Continuous Learning

Ethical AI development is not a one-time task, but an ongoing process. Innovators must commit to continuous learning and improvement, regularly assessing the impact of their AI systems and making adjustments as needed. This includes staying up-to-date with emerging ethical concerns and adapting to new regulatory frameworks.

The future of AI is a landscape filled with immense possibilities, but also significant ethical challenges. As AI technologies like Gemini AI continue to evolve, the need for ethical consideration, transparent regulation, and responsible innovation becomes more critical than ever. Innovators play a key role in shaping a future where AI is used for the greater good—benefiting society, improving lives, and enhancing our collective potential. By approaching AI development with a commitment to fairness, accountability, and responsibility, we can ensure that the technology continues to serve humanity in a way that is both ethical and beneficial for all.

Chapter 7

The Road Ahead: What's Next for Gemini AI and Tech Disruption

The advent of Gemini AI has undoubtedly marked a pivotal moment in the evolution of technology. As we stand at the threshold of a new era, the possibilities seem endless. Yet, the path forward is not just about technological advancements; it's about understanding how these innovations will reshape industries, influence society, and challenge our most fundamental assumptions about the relationship between humans and machines. The road ahead for Gemini AI and the broader world of artificial intelligence is both exciting and uncertain. This chapter explores the emerging trends in AI, what lies ahead for tech enthusiasts and innovators, and how we can prepare for the AI-powered future.

> Emerging Trends and Innovations in AI

As Gemini AI continues to push the boundaries of what is possible, it is important to consider the emerging trends and innovations that will define the next wave of artificial intelligence. AI is not a static field; it is evolving rapidly, driven by new breakthroughs in machine learning, neural networks, and computational power. The future promises a host of transformative developments that will change the way we live, work, and interact with the world around us.

1. Conversational AI and Human-Machine Interaction

One of the most significant areas of AI development is in conversational agents. The ability of AI to engage in natural, human-like conversations is rapidly advancing, and this will have profound implications for industries ranging from customer service to education and entertainment. Gemini AI, with its advanced natural language processing capabilities, represents a key milestone in this journey. But what lies ahead is an AI that can not only hold conversations but understand context, tone, and emotion at a deep level, making interactions even more fluid and meaningful. As conversational AI systems improve, we may see them take on increasingly complex roles. They could serve as virtual assistants for tasks that require emotional intelligence, such as providing psychological support or helping with decision-making in high-stakes environments. These advancements will also make AI-driven interactions more seamless, creating an experience where humans and machines collaborate effortlessly.

2. AI in Creativity and Content Generation

Another exciting frontier for AI is its role in creativity and content generation. In the past, AI has been used to automate repetitive tasks, but as the technology matures, it is now being deployed to assist in creative fields. Artists, writers, musicians, and filmmakers are using AI systems to generate ideas, design visuals, compose music, and even write scripts. Gemini AI's ability to generate ideas and creative outputs is a glimpse of the future where AI is not just a tool but a co-creator.

Moving forward, AI systems will likely become even more integrated into the creative process, offering suggestions, improving drafts, and generating entirely new forms of art and media. This democratization of creativity will open up new opportunities for individuals and small teams, giving them access to tools that were previously available only to large corporations or highly skilled professionals.

3. AI in Autonomous Systems

The realm of autonomous systems, from self-driving cars to drones and robotic process automation, is another area poised for rapid growth. While autonomous vehicles have already made their mark, the next wave will involve far more sophisticated AI systems capable of navigating even more complex environments. Gemini AI's advanced learning algorithms will be central to the development of these systems, which will not only drive cars but also manage entire fleets, optimize supply chains, and perform intricate tasks with a level of precision previously impossible. In the field of robotics, AI will enable machines to work alongside humans in more meaningful ways. These robots will not only follow commands but understand context, learn from experience, and adapt to new environments. Whether in factories, hospitals, or households, autonomous systems powered by AI will become integral parts of our everyday lives.

4. Ethical and Explainable AI

As AI continues to expand into new areas, there will be an increasing demand for transparency and accountability. One of the key areas of focus for future AI innovations is making AI systems more explainable. Currently, many AI models, including those used in Gemini AI, operate in ways that are not always transparent to the user. This "black box" problem makes it difficult for humans to understand how decisions are being made. The next steps for AI will involve developing systems that are more interpretable and understandable. This will allow users to trust AI decisions and better understand the underlying logic. Explainable AI will be crucial in fields like healthcare, finance, and law, where the stakes are high, and decisions must be made with a clear understanding of how they were arrived at.

The Next Steps for Tech Enthusiasts and Innovators

For those interested in the future of AI, whether they are developers, entrepreneurs, or industry leaders, the next steps are clear: adapt, learn, and innovate. As AI becomes increasingly embedded in every aspect of life, tech enthusiasts and innovators must stay ahead of the curve to fully realize its potential.

1. Embrace Continuous Learning

AI is advancing at an unprecedented rate, and staying informed is more important than ever. Innovators need to cultivate a mindset of continuous learning, keeping up with the latest developments in AI algorithms, machine learning frameworks, and industry applications. Those who are actively working with AI, whether in development or application, should regularly update their skill sets, exploring new tools and platforms that enable them to take full advantage of the technology.

Courses, workshops, and community-driven resources will be crucial for staying informed and improving skills. The rapid pace of AI's growth means that those who are serious about contributing to the field will need to dedicate themselves to ongoing education and adaptation.

2. Foster Cross-Disciplinary Collaboration

AI is not just a technical challenge; it is a multidisciplinary one. To push the boundaries of what AI can achieve, innovators must work together across industries, combining expertise from diverse fields such as healthcare, ethics, law, and the arts. This cross-disciplinary collaboration will be key to ensuring that AI is used effectively and responsibly.

For example, developers working on AI-driven healthcare solutions need to collaborate closely with medical professionals to understand the nuances of patient care and ensure that AI applications are safe, ethical, and effective. Similarly, those working on AI systems for autonomous vehicles must engage with regulatory bodies, urban planners, and safety experts to ensure that the technology meets the highest standards of safety and compliance.

3. Prioritize Ethical Design and Innovation

As AI systems become more pervasive, ethical design will become increasingly important. Innovators must prioritize ethics at every stage of the development process, ensuring that AI systems are transparent, fair, and accountable. This means addressing issues such as bias, privacy, and autonomy from the outset, and ensuring that AI systems are built to serve the broader good. Tech companies and startups that are at the forefront of AI innovation have a unique responsibility to lead by example. They must not only focus on the economic benefits of their technologies but also ensure that their innovations align with societal values and contribute to the well-being of all.

Preparing for the AI-Powered Future

As we look toward the future, it is clear that AI will be central to nearly every aspect of life. The challenge ahead is not just about developing new technologies, but about understanding how these technologies will reshape our world.

1. Society-Wide Engagement with AI

Preparing for an AI-powered future requires engagement from all sectors of society, not just the tech industry. Governments, educational institutions, and businesses must come together to develop frameworks for AI governance, education, and regulation. Public discourse around AI should be inclusive, involving a wide range of voices from different cultural, social, and economic backgrounds to ensure that AI technologies are developed in ways that benefit all people.

2. Reimagining Work and Employment

AI will undoubtedly impact the workforce. As automation increases, many routine jobs may be replaced, but new roles will emerge that require creative thinking, problem-solving, and human judgment. Innovators must work with governments and educational systems to ensure that workers are equipped with the skills needed to thrive in this new landscape. This could involve a shift in education towards more interdisciplinary approaches that emphasize creativity, critical thinking, and collaboration with AI systems.

3. Building Resilience

The road ahead for AI is filled with both promise and uncertainty. To prepare for this future, society must build resilience in the face of rapid technological change. This means creating adaptable systems that can evolve with AI advancements, while also ensuring that the benefits of AI are broadly shared, reducing inequality and fostering inclusivity.

The future of AI, powered by systems like Gemini AI, is a journey that holds immense promise. As we look ahead, we must not only embrace the innovations on the horizon but also carefully consider the ethical, social, and economic challenges they bring. For innovators, the path forward is one of continuous learning, responsible design, and collaboration across disciplines. For society, it is a time to engage in open dialogue and prepare for a world that is increasingly shaped by intelligent machines. The road ahead is as exciting as it is daunting, and how we navigate it will determine the kind of future we create together.

Conclusion

Charting the Future with Gemini AI

As we conclude this exploration of Gemini AI and its profound implications, we are left with a sense of both awe and responsibility. This powerful system, which has the potential to transform industries, enhance human creativity, and solve complex challenges, represents just the beginning of what AI can achieve. It is not merely a tool for automation or efficiency but a catalyst for innovation, a partner in human endeavor, and, most significantly, a driving force behind the next great leap in technological progress.

The journey of AI is one of constant evolution, and as we move forward, Gemini AI will undoubtedly play an increasingly central role in shaping the future. It has already demonstrated its potential across fields like healthcare, finance, retail, and manufacturing, with its ability to process data, generate insights, and drive decisions faster and more accurately than ever before. Yet, these applications are just the tip of the iceberg. The true potential of Gemini AI lies not just in what it can do today, but in how it will evolve and adapt to meet the needs of tomorrow. But with this potential comes the need for careful stewardship. As with any powerful technology, there are ethical challenges that must be addressed. Issues of fairness, transparency, and privacy are at the forefront of AI development, and it is incumbent upon innovators, regulators, and society at large to ensure that these systems are designed, deployed, and governed in ways that are responsible and beneficial to all. The ethical landscape surrounding AI is complex, and there will be no easy answers. However, by prioritizing accountability, equity, and transparency, we can ensure that AI serves humanity's highest ideals.

The road ahead for Gemini AI and the broader field of artificial intelligence is filled with immense opportunities—and equally formidable challenges. The next wave of innovation will not only redefine industries but will also reshape the very nature of work, creativity, and human interaction with machines. As AI continues to evolve, so too must our understanding of its implications. It is crucial for developers, entrepreneurs, and policymakers to remain adaptable, continuously learning, and anticipating the changes that will come.

For those who are ready to embrace the future, there is much to look forward to. Whether you are a developer seeking to integrate AI into your projects, a business leader hoping to harness its power to innovate, or an individual excited by the prospect of a more efficient and creative world, the opportunities are boundless. But as we stand on the threshold of an AI-powered future, we must also recognize that this future will be shaped not just by the technology itself, but by the values, choices, and responsibilities we bring to it.

In the end, the journey with Gemini AI is about more than just creating smarter machines—it is about forging a partnership between humans and technology, one that amplifies our capabilities, enhances our creativity, and drives us toward a future where technology and humanity grow together. The challenges are many, but so are the rewards. As we move forward, let us do so with a shared vision, committed to using AI to create a future that is not just smarter, but also more ethical, more inclusive, and more human.